STORIES JESUS
The Lost Sheep

CANDLE
BOOKS

Spot the Difference

Here is a farmer. He has a hundred sheep.
He is counting them.

One of his sheep is missing.
Oh dear! Where has it gone?

Is it in the hen house? No.

Is it behind the haystack? No.

Is it under the hedge?
No, it is lost.

All day the farmer looks for his sheep.
He climbs up hills and scrambles over rocks.

He crawls through bramble bushes.
The thorns scratch him.
But he does not give up.

He is tired and hungry. His feet ache.
But he does not give up.

At last, the farmer sees his sheep.
It has fallen in the river.

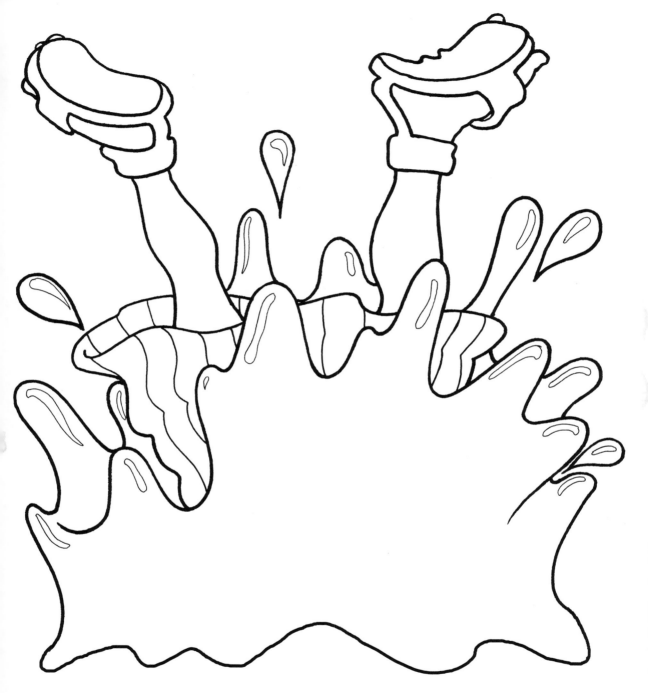

The farmer dives into the water.
Splosh! He rescues the sheep.

Hooray! The farmer has found his sheep.
'Let's all have a party,' says the farmer.

Jesus says, 'God is like the farmer.
He loves us like the farmer loves his sheep.'

STORIES JESUS TOLD
The Precious Pearl

Spot  Difference

Here is a man who buys and sells
things. He is called a merchant. He has
a fine fur coat and a felt hat with a
floppy feather. It is his favourite.

The house he lives in is huge. It has
five floors and a fishpond with a
fountain in the front garden.

The merchant has everything he wants.
He has fifteen rooms filled with furniture.

He has four freezers full of food.
(And three fridges for fizzy drinks.)

And there is more money under his mattress
than you could imagine. Much more.
Yes, the merchant has everything he wants, until…

One day, in a shop window, he sees something.
Something special. It is a wonderful white pearl.

'It costs five hundred thousand pounds,' says the man in the shop.
It is even more money than the merchant has under his mattress.
But he wants that pearl more than anything in the world.

He hurries home. He has a plan. He sells his furniture,
his fridges and his freezers full of food.
He sells his house, his fountain and his fishpond.

He sells his fine fur coat. But the felt hat with the floppy feather, he keeps. It is his favourite.

He borrows a barrow and bundles in the money.
Off to the shop he trundles to buy the pearl.

Oh dear! He is still six pounds short. 'Sell me your hat for six pounds,' says the man in the shop. The merchant laughs. He hands the man his hat and takes the pearl.

Hooray! The pearl is his at last.
Jesus says, 'God is like the merchant's pearl.
It costs everything to know him. But he is
worth more than anything in the world.'

STORIES JESUS TOLD
The Two Sons

Spot  the Difference

Here is a man.
He grows apples in an orchard.

The apples are red and rosy.
It is time for them to be picked.

At home the man has two sons.

'I want you to help me to pick the apples,'
says the man to his first son.
'No,' says the first son. 'I'm busy.'

But after a while he is sorry for what he has said.
He picks up a basket and goes to the orchard.

The man finds his second son.
'I want you to help me pick the apples too,' he says.

'I will come as soon as I have put my boots on.'

Back in the orchard the first son is busy picking apples.
Look he has already filled one basket.

'Well done son,' says the man. 'Here is another basket.
We'll have this done in no time.'

They work together until all the apples have been picked.
But there is no sign of the second son.
He has forgotten his promise.

Who do you think pleased his father?
The first son or the second son?

Jesus says, 'What we do is more
important than what we say.'

STORIES JESUS TOLD
The House On The Rock

Spot the Difference

Here is a man. He is looking for
a place to build a house.

He climbs to the top of a big grey rock.
'Ah! Here is a good place.'

The man begins to build his house on the big grey rock.
It is hard work. He puffs and pants.

He puffs and pants and grunts and groans until the work is done.
'Just in time,' he says. 'It looks like rain.'

The rain pours down. The lightning flashes. The thunder booms.
The water washes round the house and splashes at the rock.

The rock stays firm. The man
was wise to choose the rock.

Here is another man. He wants a house. He wants it now.
He wants it quick. 'Any place will do,' he says.

He builds his house down on the sand.
'This won't take long,' he says, and he
whistles as he works.

His house is done. He goes inside and
shuts the door. A raindrop drips
onto his nose. Oh dear!

The rain pours down. The lightning
flashes. The thunder booms.
The water rushes through the house
and splashes at his knees!

The sand is washed away. His house falls flat.
The silly man was wrong to build on sand.

Jesus says, 'I am like the wise man's rock.
If you trust me, I will never let you down.'

STORIES JESUS TOLD
The Ten Silver Coins

Spot  Difference

Here is a woman. She has ten silver coins.
She likes to count them. One, two, three, four...

Oops! Silly cat! Now they've gone all over the place.

The woman picks up her silver coins. They have been scattered everywhere! The cat doesn't care. He has stretched out and gone to sleep.

The woman counts her silver coins again. But there are only nine. One of them is missing! Never mind, it can't have gone far.

Perhaps it is under the rug.
No. There is no sign of it there.

Perhaps it has bounced into the fireplace.
Carefully she sifts through the ashes.
What a messy job! But no, there is no coin.

Perhaps it rolled right under the door and out into the garden.
She searches and searches, but she cannot find the coin anywhere.

She even looks inside her pots and pans,
even though she really knows it can't be there.
Clatter! Bang! What a noise she is making!

She's making so much noise,
she wakes up the cat. Serves him right.
He's off to find a quiet spot in the garden.

There it is! The cat was lying on it all the time!
The missing silver coin is found!

The woman laughs. She is so happy she
calls a friend to tell her the good news.

Jesus says, 'We are like the woman's silver coins.
God wants every single one of us.'

STORIES JESUS TOLD
The Little Gate

Spot the Difference

Here is a wall which surrounds a town.
In the wall is a little gate. It has a funny name.
It is called the Eye of a Needle because it is so small.

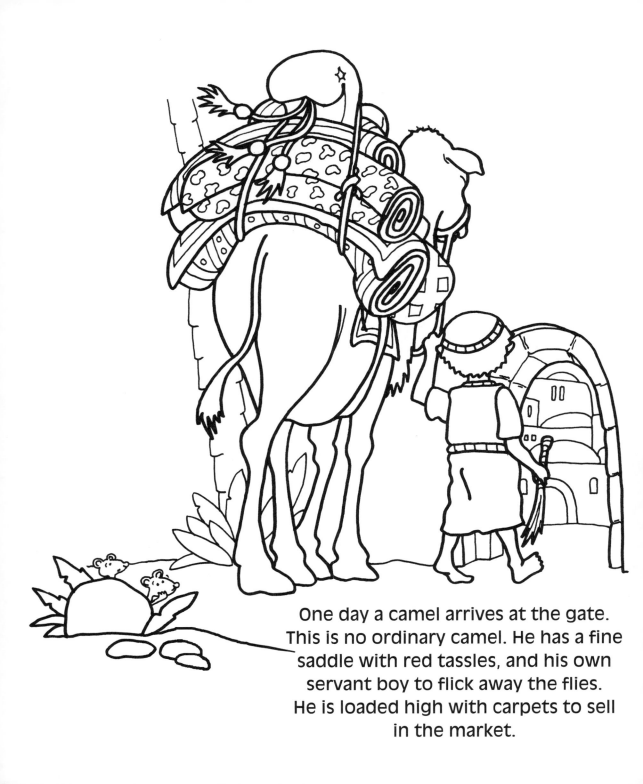

One day a camel arrives at the gate.
This is no ordinary camel. He has a fine
saddle with red tassles, and his own
servant boy to flick away the flies.
He is loaded high with carpets to sell
in the market.

'Make way,' he says 'I'm coming through!' But he isn't coming through at all! He can't get through the hole. He is too big!

'Try wriggling through backwards,' says the boy.
And he shows the camel how.

'Camels never wriggle,' says the camel. But just the same,
he turns around and pushes his bottom into the hole.

He heaves and pushes. (He even wriggles.)
But it is no good. He cannot get through the gate.

'I'll unload you,' says the boy. He unties the ropes and takes off all the carpets. 'Now try again.'

It is no use. The camel still cannot squeeze through the gate.
'Your saddle keeps getting stuck,' says the boy.
'You will have to let me take it off.'

Without his fine saddle, the camel does not look proud and important any more. He is just an ordinary camel.

Once more the camel tries. Down on his knees, shuffling forward, inch by inch, until finally...

Hooray! He is through!

Jesus says, 'It is very hard for a rich man to get into heaven. It's easier for a camel to get through the eye of a needle!'

STORIES JESUS TOLD
The Good Stranger

Spot 10 Difference

Here is a man. He is going on a long journey.
He packs some sandwiches and some water.
Then he climbs onto his donkey. 'Giddyup!'

Soon he has left the town behind him. The sun is hot and the long climb up into the hills makes his donkey puff.

The path winds between high rocks. It is a dark place,
full of shadows. 'I don't like it here,' says the man.
He has a funny feeling that someone is watching him.

Suddenly there is a shout! Robbers! Three of them!
They steal his donkey and all his belongings.
And they whack him on the head with his own stick!

Poor man. He is left lying on the path. His head is bleeding and he cannot move his legs. He lies there for a long time. Then, finally, he falls asleep.

After a while, someone comes along the path.
He is wearing fine clothes. A bishop. He stops,
then hurries past, pretending not to see.
Perhaps he is late for important business.
Perhaps he is afraid.

The man wakes up and starts to call for help.
Ah! Here comes someone. A man in a robe.
A judge. 'Help! Help!' But the judge
pretends not to hear and he hurries past.
Just like the bishop.

The sun rises high in the sky. The man is hot. His throat is dry.
But here come more footsteps! Who is it? Oh no! It is a stranger
from a foreign country. He has no friends here.
Why should he stop to help?

But the stranger does stop. He speaks kindly to the man in foreign words, and helps him to drink some water. He washes his wounds and carefully puts a bandage round his head.

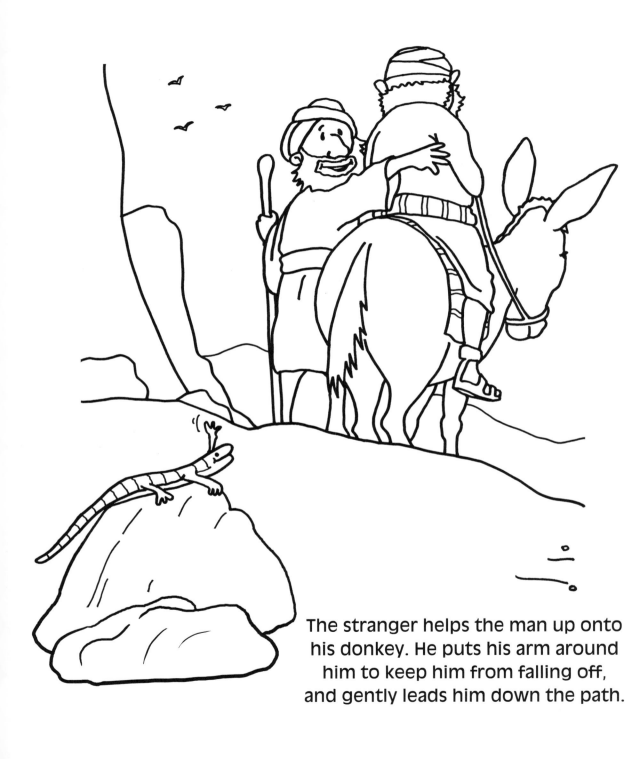

The stranger helps the man up onto
his donkey. He puts his arm around
him to keep him from falling off,
and gently leads him down the path.

At the next town the stranger finds an inn.
He puts the man to bed and pays the innkeeper.
'Look after him,' he says, 'until I get back.'

Jesus says, 'Which one was like a good neighbour?
The bishop, the judge or the stranger?'

STORIES JESUS TOLD
The Rich Farmer

Spot **10** Difference

Here is a farmer who is very rich.
The farmer is rich because his soil is rich.
And his corn grows, faster than anyone else's.

And higher than anyone else's.

And at harvest time he has much more
of it than anyone else! Lucky man.

This year he has so much corn that his old barn can't hold it all.
It is bursting at the seams.

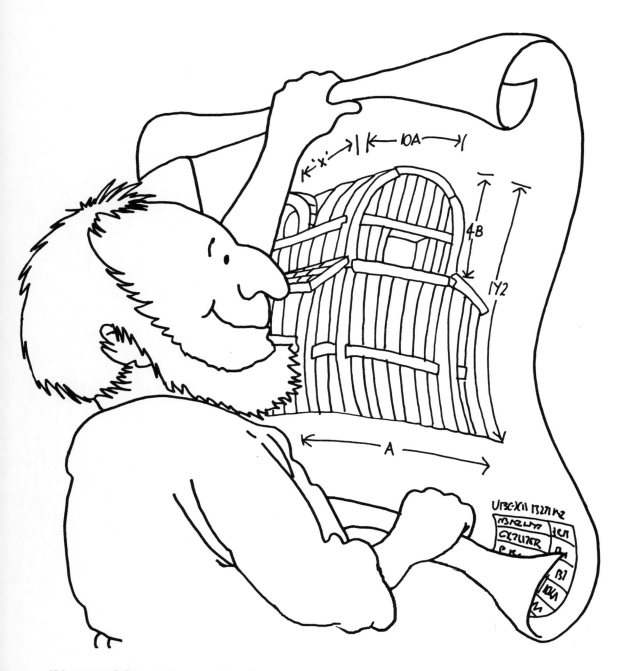

'No problem,' says the farmer. 'I will pull it down and build a bigger one. Then next year I will be rich enough to take life easy.'
So he builds a bigger barn.

But when harvest comes round again, the new barn is not big enough. The greedy farmer has planted more corn than before. And carrots too.

'No problem,' says the farmer. 'I will build an even bigger, better barn. Then next year I will be richer still and then I can really enjoy myself.' So he builds a bigger, better barn.

But at harvest time, even the bigger, better barn is not big enough. Again the farmer has planted too much corn, too many carrots. (And a few cabbages as well.)

This time, the farmer says to himself,
'I will build the biggest, grandest barn the
world has ever seen. And then I shall be so
rich, I need never work again!'

The barn he builds reaches up to the sky. When it is finished
the farmer sighs a great big sigh. 'Tomorrow I will gather in
the harvest and then at last I shall begin to enjoy myself.
I know! I'll have a party!'

But that very night he dies in his sleep. Just like that! The birds eat his corn, the rabbits dig up his carrots and his cabbages go to seed. The big barn stands empty and the rich farmer never does get to enjoy his money. Poor man.

Jesus says, 'How silly it is for a man to spend
his whole life storing up riches for himself.
To God, he is really a poor man.'